# TALL SHIPS
## The Golden Age of Sail

# TALL SHIPS
## The Golden Age of Sail

Captain John Noble

VIKING O'NEIL

Conversion Tables
One ton = 1.016 tonnes
One foot = 0.305 metres
One mile = 1.609 kilometres

Viking O'Neil
Penguin Books Australia Ltd
487 Maroondah Highway, PO Box 257
Ringwood, Victoria 3134, Australia
Penguin Books Ltd
Harmondsworth, Middlesex, England
Viking Penguin Inc.
40 West 23rd Street, New York, N.Y. 10010, U.S.A.
Penguin Books Canada Ltd
2801 John Street, Markham, Ontario, Canada L3R 1B4
Penguin Books (N.Z.) Ltd.
182-190 Wairau Road, Auckland 10, New Zealand

First published by Currey O'Neil Ross Pty Ltd 1985
as *The Golden Age of Sail*
This edition published by Penguin Books Australia Ltd 1988


Produced by Viking O'Neil
56 Claremont Street, South Yarra, Victoria 3141, Australia
A division of Penguin Books Australia Ltd

Typeset in Australia by Bookset Pty Ltd
Printed in Australia by Globe Press Pty Ltd

National Library of Australia
Cataloguing-in-Publication data

Noble, John, 1914-
Tall Ships: the golden age of sail.

Includes index.
ISBN 0 670 90106 7.

1. Sailing ships — Australasia — History.
2. Windjammers (Sailing ships). 3. Sailing ships — Australasia — History — Pictorial works. 4. Windjammers (Sailing ships) — Pictorial works. I. Title. II. Title: The golden age of sail of Australia and New Zealand.

387.2'043'099

# Contents

# The England to Australia Run

*The fair breeze blew, the white foam flew,*
*The furrow followed free;*
*We were the first that ever burst,*
*Into that silent sea.*

SAMUEL COLERIDGE
'RIME OF THE ANCIENT MARINER'

With the arrival of the First Fleet in 1788, sailing ships began to make regular voyages between England and Australia. Despite the development of steamships, windjammers continued to make 'the long haul' well into the 20th century. Carrying homeward cargoes of wheat and wool, speed was less important than operating costs. The *Pamir* and *Passat*, the last big commercial sailing ships in Australian waters, rounded Cape Horn for the final time in 1949.

Convicts came in the first ships. Emigrants and, later, cabin passengers also made the long voyage under sail. The outward passage could take four, six, even eight months. Life on board — whether in the holds of transports, in the crews' forecastles or even the cabins of elegant clippers — was cramped, tedious and fraught with danger. Ironically, disaster often struck when the rigours of the journey were almost over.

On the voyage to Australia, via the Cape of Good Hope, the North Atlantic westerlies ensured reasonable progress until the north-east trade winds were encountered near the Canary Islands, favourable for the run past the Cape Verde Islands and into the light winds and calms of the doldrums near the Equator. Here the monotony was relieved by a 'crossing the line' ceremony, a relic of pagan times when temples were erected on prominent headlands for mariners to pay homage to Neptune, lord and ruler of the seas.

Traditionally, the second mate impersonated King Neptune, attended by a 'court' including Queen Amphitrite. After appropriate initiation, first-trippers were dubbed with a wooden sword, doused with sea-water and presented with a certificate exempting the bearer from similar treatment on future voyages.

Progress through the doldrums was necessarily slow until the south-east trade winds were met. Then there would be several days of windward sailing, making a course probably slightly west of south, to the variable winds of the mid-thirty south latitudes.

By then the ship would be thirty or more days out from England and the crew would be accruing wages with the expiry of their month's pay in advance, known as the 'dead horse'. The occasion was celebrated by parading a straw-stuffed effigy of a horse round the decks before hoisting it to the yardarm to be cut down. These became known as the Horse Latitudes, progress being unpredictable until the westerlies of the Roaring Forties brought fair winds and following seas for 'running the easting down' to Australia.

It was here that navigation by right-angled plane trigonometry along rhumb lines gave way to great circle sailing and spherical trigonometry. Great circles are circles on a sphere, the plane of which passes through the centre of the sphere. On east-west courses in high latitudes a considerable saving in distance could be achieved by following the curve towards the pole of great circles, into the even stronger westerlies of the higher latitudes. This exposed ships to additional hazards in the form of extreme cold, icebergs and violent storms.

Shipmasters had to assess the advantage of the shorter distance against these added risks, and decide upon a maximum latitude by using composite courses: the great circle to the maximum latitude, due east along this parallel until the great circle was again intersected, and thence along the great circle north-eastwards to the landfall.

Position-fixing when making a landfall was all important. Latitude was found by meridian altitudes of the sun; longitude by chronometer, an accurate timepiece kept on Greenwich time. Both depended upon good visibility, but skies were often overcast in the high south latitudes and navigators had to rely on deduced reckoning: courses steered by compass and distance run by log. Unpredictable currents added to the uncertainty.

Furthermore, chronometers and compasses were liable to acquire an unknown error during the long voyage, which could create another uncertainty when making the landfall. Ships that were east of their estimated longitude approaching Bass Strait on the final north-easterly leg of their great circle course would be too close to the inhospitable western shore of King Island; those that were west of estimated longitude were heading for the rugged Otway coast where the *Loch Ard* was wrecked.

Although there were landfall lighthouses on Cape Otway and King Island, as well as in the approaches to Investigator Strait for the Adelaide-bound ships' landfall, these only lessened the chance of shipwreck.

Homeward-bound from Australia via Cape Horn, the great circle track goes well into the Antarctic. It was usual for ship-masters to follow a great circle course to the latitude of Cape Horn and to maintain this latitude to that cape. From the northern tip of Tasmania this course passed well south of New Zealand and close to the mist-enshrouded and uninhabited Auckland and Campbell islands. Many ships on this route were never heard of again. Some were known to have been wrecked on the off-lying islands, while others survived after running into icebergs.

Captain Hunter, pioneering the Cape Horn route in HMS *Sirius* in 1789, gave only an inkling of such perils when he recorded: 'fresh gales and hazy and cold weather . . . passed several very large and high islands of ice, had frequent squalls of hail and snow . . . we were 28 days floating with these lumps of misery in sight . . .'

Those fortunate enough to get round the Horn made a north-westerly course in the South Atlantic to pick up the south-east trades and then north through the doldrums to the north-east trades and west of north, to take advantage of the Gulf Stream and the North Atlantic westerlies, to their destination.

Whale oil and sealskins were Australia's first export cargoes. After the Third Fleet arrived at Port Jackson in 1791, Enderby Brothers of London chartered three of the transports as South Sea whalers. Emancipated First Fleet convicts, James Underwood and Henry Kable, started whaling out of Sydney in 1800. In 1806 merchant seaman William Collins began whaling operations in Van Diemen's Land, using the recently-established port of Hobart as his headquarters. By the 1860s Hobart was the most important deep-sea whaling base in the British Empire. However, by this time wool, wheat, coal and other minerals had become the principal Australian exports.

Nineteenth-century gold rushes in California and Victoria contributed to the development of racing clipper ships. In about the middle of the century, American clippers took prospectors from the eastern states to the Californian goldfields, sailing westwards round Cape Horn. With the repeal of the British Navigation Act, they were able to cross the Pacific to compete with British Blackwall frigates for tea cargoes homewards. When gold was discovered in Victoria, clippers raced to the ports of Melbourne and Geelong, carrying fortune-hunters and supplies, and returning with wheat and wool.

Tea clippers were a development of the opium clippers; both carried compact and valuable — if disreputable — cargo, and consequently required sufficient speed to evade pirates and revenue cutters. Blackwall frigates were the British version of the tea clipper. Originally built at Blackwall on the Thames in 1837, they were round and full in the bow above the waterline, but sharp as a wedge below, with a long, flat floor and a clean run aft. Their lines were finer than those of the East Indiamen, and their rig similar to that of naval frigates: square-rigged on three masts with a single deck. Blackwall frigates were later employed on the England to Australia passenger and cargo run, and recorded fast passages.

The 700-ton *Rainbow* is generally regarded as the first of the American clippers. Built at New York in 1845, she had a long sharp entrance, concave at the bow, maximum beam abaft of amidships, and a clean run towards the stern. Foremost of the American clipper builders was Donald MacKay of Boston, who improved the design of ships intended for the Californian, Chinese and Australian trades. Most of the record passages to Australia were made by British-owned, American-built ships: outwards with emigrants and homewards with Australian wool or China tea.

As shipbuilding timber, abundant in North America, became scarce in England, British shipbuilders turned to iron construction. In 1784 Henry Cort had invented a puddling process that enabled the production of iron in plates and bars. The first iron vessels were canal barges. The first sea-going iron ship was built at Liverpool in 1815. The *Garry Owen*, built at Birkenhead in 1834, was the first to have transverse iron bulkheads.

Several more iron ships had been built by 1838 when iron was chosen to build the huge steamship, the *Great Britain*, for the trans-Atlantic run. Completed in 1843, she was 322 feet long with a beam of 50 feet on a draught of 18 feet, with five watertight iron bulkheads.

The tremendous strength of iron ships was proved when, after five trans-Atlantic voyages, the *Great Britain* ran aground on the Irish coast and was exposed to the elements for ten months without sustaining serious damage. She was later bought for the Australian trade. Converted into an auxiliary steamship, the original five masts were replaced by the traditional full-rigged ship rig: square-sails on three masts.

There is an interesting postscript to this old iron mammoth. In 1968, after more than seventy years as a rusty hulk in Port Stanley, English philanthropist Jack Hayward donated £300 000 to return the *Great Britain* to her namesake country. In April 1970 she was brought back to the Bristol drydock in which she had been built more than a century earlier. She is now being restored, to the original plans, for posterity.

Composite construction — wooden planking over an iron frame — was adopted by British shipbuilders in answer to the American clipper ship challenge. Between 1863 and 1879 most of the ships were composite. The *Sobraon*, built in 1866 by Halls of Aberdeen, was the largest. Designed for the China tea trade she ended her life on the Australian run after the Suez Canal was opened.

Iron ships inevitably led to iron masts and spars and wire rigging, considerably heavier and stronger than the wooden spars and hempen rigging previously used. Running before the gales and greybeards of the Southern Ocean, these sturdy iron ships could be driven hard and were less likely to broach to, but rigging and spars could thus be tested to the limit, and dismastings were not uncommon.

Eventually, steamships using the Suez Canal eliminated the horrors of the Southern Ocean for passengers, but wool and wheat cargoes continued to be shipped in windjammers. Fast passages were less important than operating costs which were held in check by reduced manning scales. Full-rigged ships were cut back to barques by removing the square-sails from the mizzen mast, thereby reducing sail handling by about one-third. Most big sailing ships from 1880 onwards were three- or four-masted barques.

At this time, steamships needed coaling stations wherever they went, and it was sailing ships that were used to supply the coal. There was also an increasing demand for coal gas. With an abundance of good steaming and gas coal available at Newcastle, New South Wales, sailing ships converged there to await their turn at the loading berths.

Ballast disposal was a big problem for sailing ships. In the clipper ship days, washed shingle was used as ballast and kept aboard when lightly-weighted wool and tea cargoes were carried. Wheat and coal and other minerals being shipped from Australia were deadweight. Ballast necessary for outward voyages had to be unloaded and disposed of at the shipowners' expense. Sand, shingle or rubble could be dumped or unloaded in port but both operations were time consuming and labour intensive.

Before the turn of the century, outward-bound sailing ships carried such commodities as building bricks and slates as ballast. Disposal price at the destination might only offset the handling costs, but this was preferable to no return and accounts for the extensive use of imported slates for roofing houses in Australia at that time.

As the 20th century progressed, more and more cargoes were lost to steamships where there were no ballast problems. Salt water was carried in double-bottom tanks for this purpose. Sailing ships sought low-profit outward cargoes such as nitrates and phosphate rock to avoid ballasting. However, big iron barques with lofty masts were top-heavy when empty and had to load some outward cargo before discharging all their ballast or inward cargo to maintain stability.

At a time when the age of sail was drawing to a close, Captain Gustaf Erikson of Mariehamn, Finland, began buying up sailing ships. After World War 1, several of the remaining sailing ships under the German flag were surrendered as reparations for U-boat losses, but were found to have been wilfully damaged and were not recommissioned before the post-war boom ended. Captain Erikson snapped up several of these at scrap-metal prices, operating them outwards to Australia with whatever cargoes were offering, and homewards with wheat.

Three of Erikson's ships survived World War 2: the *Lawhill*, *Pamir* and *Passat*. The *Lawhill*, the last big sailing ship to visit Melbourne in 1943, was abandoned as a derelict on the east coast of Africa not long afterwards. The *Pamir* and *Passat* loaded their last wheat cargoes from Australia in 1949.

By early this century, training in sailing ships was becoming difficult because of the few opportunities. Several of the last to be built were either designed as, or converted into, training ships. Most of them came to Australia to either load wheat or wool. Later, when Captain Erikson was the only commercial sailing ship operator, there were boys from all seafaring countries seeking opportunities to train in sail. Captain Erikson accepted likely lads who had little thought about remuneration, and were willing to put up with the arduous life.

In 1908, the Union Steamship Company of New Zealand acquired two sail training ships: the three-masted barques, the *Dartford* and *Loch Lomond*. Unfortunately the latter foundered on her delivery voyage, but the *Dartford* sailed the seven seas for four years, manned by young New Zealanders, before being hulked at Wellington. During the post-war shipping boom, from 1918 to 1921, she was recommissioned and ended her days as a coal hulk at Auckland. Another former hulk, the *Countess of Anglesea*, renamed the *Gladbrook*, was recommissioned as a three-masted barque at the same time.

The Union Steamship Company's expertise in operating sailing ships stood the company in good stead when Erikson's four-masted barque, the *Pamir*, arrived at Wellington in 1941, with a cargo of guano from the Seychelles. Britain having decided that Finland was enemy-occupied territory, the *Pamir* was seized as a war prize. For the next seven years some fortunate New Zealand lads were the last to be able to train in sail under the British flag.

JOHN NOBLE

EXCELSIOR
LAURVIK

# Life at Sea

'No man will be a sailor who has contrivance enough to get himself into a jail; for being in a ship is being in a jail, with the chance of being drowned . . . A man in a jail has more room, better food, and commonly better company.'

This ironic observation by 18th century writer and wit Dr Samuel Johnson carried much truth. The life of a seaman was one of constant danger and discomfort, combined with long hours and low pay. The 'chance of being drowned' was very high in the 1880s when one in ten British ships was lost at sea, and one in twenty crewmen lost his life.

When rounding Cape Horn seamen often had to battle their way across decks swept by swirling, icy seas — a rope lifeline their only security. Topmen had the even more treacherous task of straddling the yards after climbing the creaking masts via the 'ratlines' to secure the sails. In freezing, gale-force winds and turbulent seas this was an heroic task.

The strong sense of camaraderie which existed between men was heightened by stirring sea-shanties, of which 'Rolling Home' and 'Haul on the Bowline' were two of the oldest. There were capstan shanties, for the steady efforts needed on the capstan bars, and halyard shanties, with the accent on occasional notes when all had to pull together. Words of shanties varied from ship to ship and were improvised to keep the singing going until the task was finished.

Men were often drenched on the job, and there were few facilities for drying clothes on the long haul across the Southern Ocean. Often the only answer was to sleep in wet garments.

Living quarters were spartan. Regulations demanded only twelve square feet of accommodation per man; neither messrooms nor tables were provided. The men had to bring their own utensils: usually a knife, fork and spoon, a tin plate and a 'hook-pot': a pannikin with a lid and hooks by which it could be attached to the bunkboard when not in use. Each man usually made his own sea-chest, sometimes brass-bound, with artwork inside the lid and decorative ropework handles. Kit bags filled with soft clothing doubled as pillows and two coarse blankets supplemented the straw-filled 'donkey's breakfast' for bedding. Forecastle accommodation, as the name implies, was traditionally in the eyes of the ship, but in later years many ships were built with a 'Liverpool house' abaft of the foremast. Abaft of the mainmast — the quarterdeck — was the officers' domain.

Despite the dangers and deprivations, life at sea provided adventure and the chance to see the world, and there was never any shortage of eager recruits.

The Norwegian barque the *Excelsior* is 'running the easting down', under the command of Captain Bronlund who is standing between lifelines, clad in his weatherproof Cape Horn suit. The two helmsmen are wearing safety harnesses to prevent them from being washed overboard.

Apprentices were taken on to 'learn the ropes' at a tender age. The barefooted boy on this unidentified windjammer looks little more than twelve, while the two lads seated in the foreground would be in their early teens. Mutual understanding between masters, mates, men and boys was essential to the smooth running of a ship. More experienced crew members passed on their seafaring skills to apprentices and deckboys. This crew is made up of quite a mixture of nationalities.

Some of the crew of the *Speculant,* the largest ship ever registered at Warrnambool, Victoria, pose in their shore-going attire, the master and mates in hard hats. Most ships carried cats to keep down the rats, and the *Speculant's* cat is included in this group. On 11 February 1911 the *Speculant* was wrecked on the Otway coast while on passage from Portland to Melbourne. Fortunately, all hands survived by scrambling across rocks to safety.

The captain's wife sometimes accompanied him on voyages. No doubt her presence provided a softening influence on an otherwise ruggedly male domain. Here the captain and his wife and child pose with two mates and two apprentices on a Tasmanian barque in the 1890s.

Sailors had to be self-sufficient and to provide their own amusements. Here some of the crew of the 358-ton intercolonial barque *Mananui* are at leisure in port; they read and smoke pipes while the youngest makes a model under the watchful gaze of an elder.

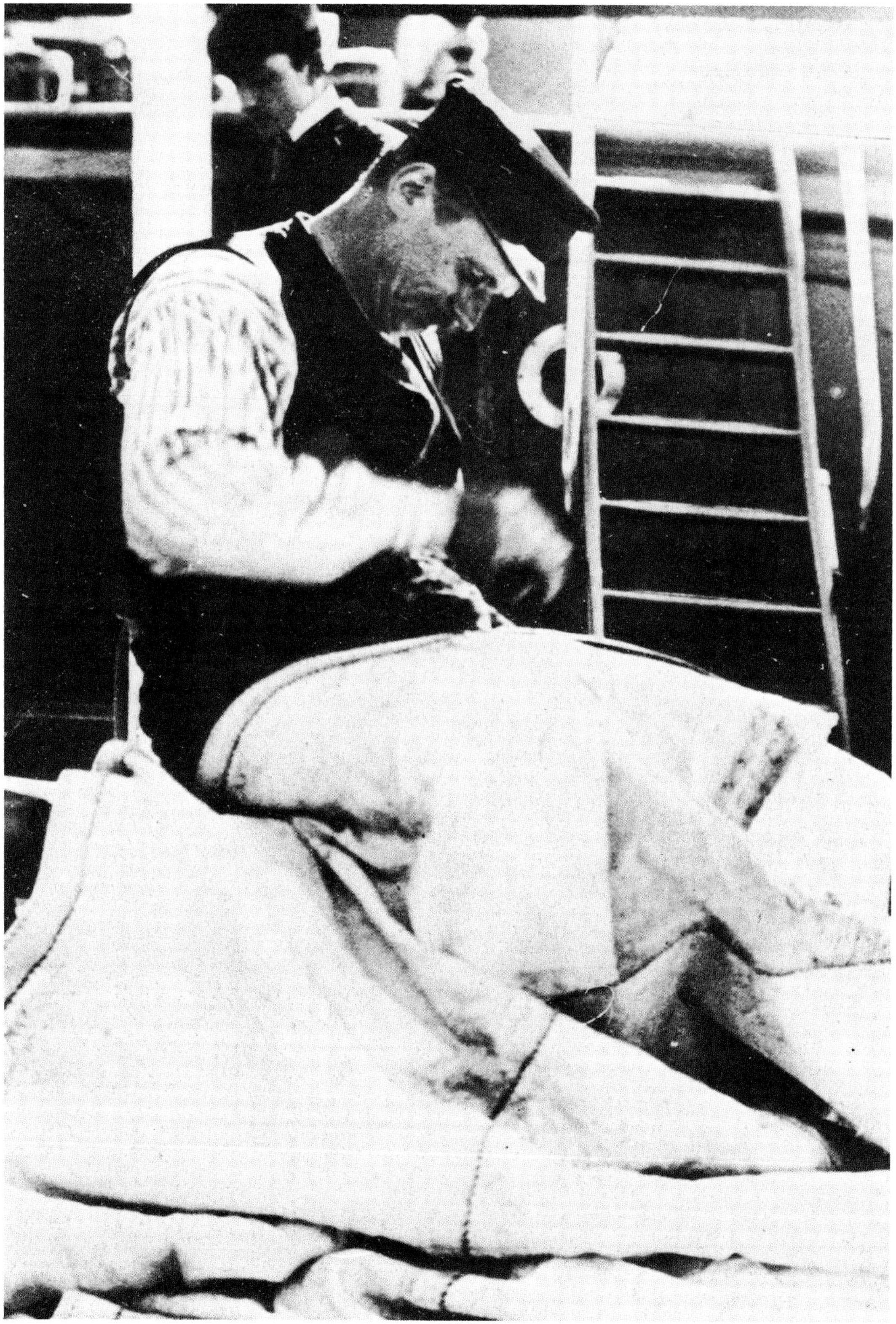

To stand up to gale-force winds, sails had to be patched and repaired constantly. This was the job of the sailmaker or 'sails', but most crewmen could turn their hands to skilful repair jobs. The man in the photo, probably one of the mates, wields the 'palm and needle' to repair a sail, which he has tucked under his buttocks in the correct manner. The palm was a leather strap which went round the hand, with a metal fitting used to push the long, three-cornered needle through the tough canvas.

A flock of albatrosses resting aboard the *Arctic Stream* seems to sense the old sailors' superstition that it is unlucky to kill these large seabirds. The *Arctic Stream*, a 1584-ton ship built in 1885, was well known on the Australian run for speedy passages. One of her records was from San Francisco to Sydney in 64 days. In the Southern Ocean albatrosses followed ships for weeks.

When sailing ships reached the Equator a 'crossing the line' ceremony relieved the monotony of the light winds and calms of the doldrums. Traditionally the second mate, dressed as King Neptune and attended by his court, initiated first-trippers in a boisterous ceremony. After being doused with sea-water, they were presented with a certificate. This photograph was taken aboard the *Carmanian*, a steel barque built in 1894.

This photograph emphasises the size of the wheel. It required considerable strength to turn, and in bad weather required two men, who stood on the small platforms on either side. In really heavy seas the men would be lashed to the wheel to prevent them from being washed overboard. This photograph was taken aboard the *Dimsdale,* 'the ship which sank a lighthouse'. In November 1912 she ran into the Wonga Shoal lighthouse outside Port Adelaide, knocking it down. The two unfortunate lighthouse-keepers were drowned.

Every task on a sailing ship had to be performed with the utmost skill and efficiency. This photograph of men preparing a sail for hoisting to the yard was taken aboard the *Bertha,* a variously-named four-masted barque originally owned in Liverpool. Under the German flag as the *Bertha* she was commandeered by the Americans in World War 1.

In square-rigged ships maximum sailing ability was obtained by trimming the braces — tackles attached to the ends of yards. That on the lee side of the foresail yard was particularly important, the order, 'Lee fore brace!', demanding immediate attention when the watch-keeping officer considered an adjustment necessary. Sails were furled or reefed when the wind increased. Deckmen had to know every halyard and running rigging. Here the 358-ton *Mananui* ploughs through the sea at a good pace. This small wooden ship, built in Denmark in 1896, was sold to Sydney owners in 1912.

Here the *Mananui* runs before the wind while the crew mans the foresail braces and sheets. Life on sailing ships was made up of long hours, low pay, frequent danger and much discomfort. Men often got soaked through and, in bad weather, the only way to dry their clothes was to sleep in them. Despite this, the romance of life at sea ensured a constant supply of eager recruits.

In this photograph of the *Mananui* some of the crew scale the mainmast to take in the mainsail. The foresail and topsails are set and the mizzen furled. Weather is fine with a gentle breeze from the starboard quarter.

On the outward voyage sailing ships used the prevailing westerlies of the Roaring Forties to carry them eastwards to Australia. Here Captain L. Concord takes a determined stance as he weathers rough seas on the poop of the *State of Maine* as she 'runs the easting down', south of the Cape of Good Hope. This 1546-ton wooden ship was owned in Maine, USA. The whirling of the patent taffrail log governor, attached to the clock for recording distance run (near the captain's left leg), indicates that the ship is making at least ten knots.

Topmen had to climb aloft up the ratlines — steps attached to the standing rigging — and, on reaching the yard, out along the footropes: ropes under the yard supported at intervals by stirrups. With their bodies bent over the yard, they secured the sail. This was particularly hazardous in heavy weather, as in this photograph of the *Garthsneid,* taken off Cape Horn in 1904. Men lost overboard through falling from aloft had little chance of rescue when the ship was running before a gale, but after sail had been reduced conditions on deck became better, and the ship easier to handle. There was less likelihood of dismasting or loss of gear through failure of sails or rigging.

Few funerals could be more moving — or bleak — than the simple ceremony which took place when a sailor died at sea. Seamen gathered to hear the master perform a short service before lowering the body of their shipmate into the deep. The risk of death was ever-present on long sea voyages. A ship's doctor was a luxury reserved for ships carrying more than 50 people. This photograph was taken aboard the *Loch Tay,* one of a fleet of big iron barques owned by the Loch Line of Glasgow.

Wild, foaming seas lashed by gales submerge the deck of the *Passat* as she rounds the Horn. Conditions like these were commonplace on this part of the voyage, and the crew had to carry out orders regardless. The only concession to the weather was the lifelines, which sailors clung to as they battled their way across the deck. The *Passat* was one of the last big commercial sailing ships in Australian waters.

# Shipwrecks

The treacherous Australian coast is literally littered with the wrecks of sailing ships. The long stretch from Cape Leeuwin on the south-western tip of Western Australia to the eastern seaboard, was a challenge many ships failed to meet. With few recognisable land-marks, ships could all too easily founder, despite the combined experience, bravery and skill of their masters and men. With only the most basic navigational equipment and no reserves of power, sailing ships were at the mercy of sudden changes of weather, poor visibility, lashing gales or treacherous tide rips. Uncharted rocks and reefs were an additional hazard.

After surviving the Roaring Forties, the worst part of the voyage still awaited: the horrors of Bass Strait, straddled by the rocks and reefs of King Island. Between 1835 and 1877, twenty-three ships were wrecked on King Island, with a loss of more than 800 lives.

To make matters worse, some unscrupulous shipowners shamelessly overloaded (and over-insured) their ships, recovering ample compensation if they foundered in heavy weather. Shipowners did not have to account for the loss of life of their unfortunate crews.

In 1873 Samuel Plimsoll helped to rectify this situation by producing a booklet entitled *Our Seamen.* A subsequent royal commission recommended action, and in 1876 the Merchant Shipping Act was amended to require a loadline to be painted on every ship's side. To this day it is known as the Plimsoll line.

Courts of marine inquiry were set up, with the power to cancel or suspend the certificates of competency of masters and mates deemed to be at fault. Speculation on the fate of the many ships that disappeared without trace could be based only on the evidence of those who survived similar voyages.

As a result of the findings of these courts, lighthouses and other aids to navigation were established. Undoubtedly these helped to save some ships, but shipwrecks continued to occur.

Ironically, after the rigours of the long voyage from England through the stormy seas of the Roaring Forties, many sailing ships were wrecked within a few miles of their destination. As this photograph and those on the following pages so graphically demonstrate, many sailing ships were driven ashore along Australia's inhospitable coastline. In such cases the crew and passengers often managed to scramble to safety. Sometimes stranded ships were later successfully refloated to resume their life at sea. When this proved impossible, cargo and movable fixtures might be salvaged before the ship was finally broken up by the sea. Here surf lashes the *Hereward,* a 1513-ton iron ship that was blown ashore at Maroubra Beach in the May gales of 1895, while making for Sydney Harbour.

The *Hereward* remained at Maroubra until the following December when a successful bid was made to refloat her. Unfortunately, just as she was being towed out to sea, a southerly blew up, her towline parted and she drifted back to the beach and was wrecked. Here workmen prepare to refloat the ship, with the help of sliprails, cables and sandbags.

Two small children pose on Stockton Beach beside the *Durisdeer*, a 989-ton barque that became grounded on 22 December 1895 while attempting to enter Newcastle, New South Wales, under tow. The township of Stockton, now a suburb, is separated from Newcastle by the mouth of the Hunter River.

When the tide went out the *Durisdeer* rolled over on her side, making salvage operations impossible. Fortunately, there was no loss of life although the ship became a total wreck. The *Durisdeer*, chartered to load coal for South America, was launched at Glasgow as the *City of Lahore*.

The *County Antrim*, a 1200-ton barque, sprang a serious leak while passing through Bass Strait in June 1897. This was caused by her cargo of steel rails shifting. Captain Hyland elected to run his ship up on the Victorian coastline at Ninety Mile Beach, eight kilometres west of Lakes Entrance. All hands managed to get ashore, but the *County Antrim* was soon buried in the sand and declared a total loss. At the court of marine inquiry it was suggested that if the captain had signalled for assistance in the moderating weather his ship might have been saved. Here sightseers watch the grounded ship from the shore. Two men can be seen on board, possibly attempting salvage operations.

The remains of the *George Roper*, a 2033-ton iron barque, still lie in the shallow water near the reef off Point Lonsdale, Victoria, where she was wrecked in the early hours of 4 July 1884, while attempting to enter Port Phillip. Built only a year before, the *George Roper* was in tow to the paddle steamer *Williams* when she struck the reef. Efforts to refloat her proved fruitless and lighters were sent to take the cargo on to Melbourne. Most fittings were recovered before she broke up a few weeks later. Another new ship, the 2203-ton *Holyhead,* carrying a similar cargo from Liverpool, was wrecked on the same reef about seven years later, on 12 February 1890. Among the *Holyhead's* crew rescued by the Queenscliff lifeboat was a seaman who had also been in the *George Roper.*

More large ships have been lost along Victoria's Otway coast, west of Port Phillip Heads, than on any other part of the Australian coastline. Among them was the majestic *Falls of Halladale*, a 2000-ton, four-masted barque bound for Melbourne from New York. As she approached Cape Otway, in the early hours of 14 November 1908, the helmsman sighted land but did not tell anyone. Half an hour later both the second mate and the boatswain reported their sightings to the captain, who was still perusing his chart when the ship grounded on the aptly-named Wreck Reef, 50 kilometres west of Cape Otway. The crew of 29 reached the shore safely, but attempts to salvage the barque failed. For the following two months, until the ship broke up, the adjacent coast became a popular place for picnicking sightseers. With sails set, the *Falls of Halladale* provided a magnificent spectacle. A subsequent court of inquiry deemed the captain to have been negligent for not taking soundings when approaching land, and for not putting the barque about when land was sighted. His first mate was reprimanded for his statement that there was too much to do in a sailing ship to waste time taking soundings. The second mate must have liked his new surroundings; he gave up his seafaring life to settle in the area.

One of the most 'popular' wrecks of the day was that of the *Vincennes*, a 2311-ton barque that ran aground on Ocean Beach at Sydney's North Shore suburb of Manly on 24 May 1906. Specially-run 'moonlight' cruises were conducted by the local ferry company, attracting about 70 000 sightseers, and making a small fortune for the company. On 2 June two tugs finally managed to pull her free. After being towed to Port Jackson for repairs, the *Vincennes* eventually resumed her career for another fifteen years, before being laid up in 1921 and finally broken up in 1926.

The lonely, rusting hull of the *Ethel* is testimony to the durability of iron sailing ships. This 711-ton Norwegian barque was driven ashore on the beach below Reef Head on Yorke Peninsula, South Australia, on 2 January 1904. One of the crew attempted to swim ashore with a line but was swept out to sea by an undertow and drowned. Ironically, the next morning the seas were calm enough for the rest of the crew to wade to safety. In April an attempt to refloat the *Ethel* failed when a sudden storm snapped the tow line, and she was driven back high on the beach where she remains to this day. A monument featuring one of her anchors has been erected on the cliffs above.

The ketch *Wanderer*, the schooner *Duke of Edinburgh* and the brig *Fairy Queen* were driven ashore in a gale at Timaru, New Zealand, on 27 August 1873. The *Fairy Queen*, pictured, a 214-ton wooden brig built in 1863 for Melbourne shipowner George Nipper, was driven ashore when her anchor cable parted. After striking rocks the brig was thrown up on to the beach and wrecked. Her crew of nine survived.

Eight men died and two were injured in this incident involving the *Ben Venue* and the *City of Perth* at Timaru in 1882. Early in the morning of 14 May the *Ben Venue* rolled heavily in the onshore swell, shifting her cargo of coal. In deteriorating weather the anchors dragged and eventually the cables parted as the ship was driven ashore broadside to the breaking seas, listing heavily to port. The crew sought refuge aboard the *City of Perth* which was anchored nearby. However she too had to be abandoned when her anchors dragged and she grounded close to the *Ben Venue*, head to sea on an even keel. The harbour master, Captain Mills, went out in a whaleboat manned by local watermen, but got into difficulties. The Timaru lifeboat was then launched but capsized. It was not until the following morning that the full extent of the disaster was realised. Captain Mills had died soon after arriving home, the second mate and the carpenter of the *City of Perth* and five of the local watermen had been drowned, and the *Ben Venue* was a total wreck, with two of her crew badly hurt. The *City of Perth* was refloated and renamed *Turakina*. Another ship, the *City of Cashmere* had been wrecked at Timaru exactly four months earlier. All three ships were built at Glasgow in the 1860s.

Tom Pearce and Eva Carmichael, both aged nineteen, were the sole survivors of one of Australia's best-known shipwrecks, that of the *Loch Ard.* This 1693-ton iron ship, one of the 'Unlucky Loch Line', was wrecked on Victoria's notoriously treacherous Otway coast on 1 June 1878. The captain, who had been unable to fix his position for several days because of hazy conditions, estimated that the ship was 150 nautical miles south-west of Cape Otway. In fact, it was much closer, and at nightfall struck a rocky islet at the cliff base. The first lifeboat launched capsized, drowning four sailors as it drifted shorewards, with apprentice Tom Pearce trapped underneath. The passengers and crew were swept to their death as the ship broke up. Eva Carmichael, the only passenger to survive, clung to a floating hen coop and was later dragged ashore by Tom. When he resumed his apprenticeship on the *Loch Sunart*, he survived another shipwreck off the Irish coast the following year.

One of Tom Pearce's sons, another Tom Pearce, was among the crew of the 1485-ton *Loch Vennachar* which was lost with all hands. It was last seen approaching the Investigator Strait, off South Australia, in September 1905. Wreckage was found in what is now known as Vennachar Bay on Kangaroo Island. Ironically, in 1899, Captain Bennett of the *Loch Vennachar* had suggested the landfall lighthouse on South Neptune Island, in order to improve the facilities for ships approaching Investigator Strait. It is little wonder that the Loch Line of Glasgow was called the 'Unlucky Loch Line'. Between 1873 and 1922 at least sixteen of the company's ships disappeared, were wrecked, caught fire or were lost in enemy action in World War 1. Those which perished in Australasian waters included the *Loch Maree*, *Loch Fyne*, *Loch Sloy*, *Loch Long*, *Loch Leven*, *Loch Lomond*, as well as the *Loch Ard* and the *Loch Vennachar*.

NORTH SHORE

# In Port

In the days when sailing ships were the only link between Australia and the 'Mother Country', the wharves of every capital city thronged with life. Ships not only carried much-needed cargoes, they also brought passengers and precious news from home in the form of letters and journals.

Local newspapers devoted their front pages to the arrivals and departures of ships. On Sundays sightseers swarmed to gaze at the towering masts of the stately vessels, and to capture some vicarious excitement.

Ships stayed in port for some weeks, not only to unload outward cargoes and load homeward ones, but so that masts, spars and rigging, inevitably damaged by the rigours of the long voyage, could be repaired or renewed. Hulls were inspected in drydock. Finally, when ships were ready to sail, fresh water and food were taken on for the next voyage.

Long stays in port helped to restore the health and good spirits of the crew who had often been confined for 100 days or more in cramped quarters. Some men found conditions in port too satisfying, and did not make the return voyage.

The older sections of many Australian ports, such as the steep streets and steps of Sydney's Rocks area or of Hobart's Battery Point, retain the atmosphere of the days when they were rollicking maritime villages, with an inn on every corner.

Ships continued to be the lifeline between the colonies and the outside world well into the 20th century, until the development of aviation. Ports are still vital and busy centres for the loading and unloading of imports and exports, but they lack the life and colour of the days of sail, when they bristled with forests of tall masts, and thronged with customs officers, passengers and sailors from the four corners of the earth.

Circular Quay, Sydney, in its heyday as a bustling port. The famous wool clipper *Cutty Sark* is tied up near the North Shore ferry terminal while the higgledy-piggledy streets of The Rocks, a sailor's paradise of inns, brothels and sly-grog shops, can be seen beyond.

By the end of the 19th century, wool was the main homeward cargo for sailing ships in Australian ports. In this photograph of Circular Quay in 1870 Mort's wool store, with its famous sheep emblem, dominates the waterfront. Wool from Mort & Co. was loaded on to ships berthed at the south-eastern corner of the quay. Next to the warehouse is the Belmore Family Hotel, which would have been a welcome sight for seamen after the toils and dangers of their long months at sea. No doubt the scene of much roistering, it was later better known as the First and Last. Situated in one of the finest harbours in the world, Sydney Cove was chosen as the site for settlements in 1788 because of the fresh water available from the long-vanished Tank Stream. At first some of the wharves in Sydney Cove were privately owned. From 1871 until the turn of the century the port was administered by the Marine Board of New South Wales. Then the Sydney Harbour Trust took over all privately-owned wharves and their operations. In 1936 the Maritime Services Board was established to adminsiter the affairs of all New South Wales ports.

Much development had taken place by the time this photograph was taken from east Circular Quay, not far from where the Opera House now stands. Mort's greatly extended warehouses still dominate the quay, dwarfing the Customs House on their right. Several landmarks which have survived to the present can be seen, including the graceful Customs House, the Manly and North Shore ferry wharves and the unfinished GPO clock tower, no longer visible from this viewpoint.

This view of Circular Quay is from Dawes Point where the southern pylon of the Sydney Harbour Bridge now stands. In 1878 Dawes Point became a makeshift fort as a result of fears of Russian invasion. The cannon in the foreground is one of several which were placed in position ready to fire on any enemy ship that entered Port Jackson.

Fitted out as a convict transport, the *Success* proved a popular if slightly macabre attraction for the people of Sydney when she was tied up at Circular Quay in 1891. Built in 1840, the *Success* brought gold prospectors to the Victorian port of Geelong in 1852. Having been deserted by the crew, who rushed off to try their luck on the goldfields, she was later bought by the government to be used for much-needed prison accommodation. The *Success*, one of three similar ships moored off Williamstown, housed 119 prisoners, many of whom were manacled in solitary confinement. Floggings took place on deck. Prison hulks were abandoned when Melbourne's Pentridge Prison was enlarged. The *Success* lay idle until 1880 when she was sold to be fitted as a pseudo convict transport. Her money-making spree, which took her right round the world, ended in North America. She caught fire on Lake Erie in July 1946.

Hobart's harbour matched Sydney's for size and safety, and by 1820 was competing with Sydney for overseas trade. However, at this time, Hobart lacked Sydney's port facilities. In the early years passengers were landed on Hunter's Island and carried ashore. In 1834 a stone quay was built along Battery Point. When this was extended to become New Wharf (now Prince's Wharf) Hunter's Island was reclaimed. In this early view of Hobart three well-known ships are tied up. They are (from left) the *Helen* and *Asia*, both whalers, and the intercolonial trader, *Wild Wave*.

Coal was one of the last cargoes sailing ships could economically carry. Ironically, as steam began to replace sail, many fine sailing ships ended their days carrying bunker coal to fuel steamships. Here the graceful *Chittagong*, once a luxurious passenger liner, waits at Newcastle, New South Wales, to be loaded with coal. By 1900, when this photograph was taken, she was operating under another name: *Arundel Castle*. Newcastle soon became the second port of New South Wales. This was due to its situation at the mouth of the Hunter River which runs through the Hunter Valley's rich, alluvial plains, with their extensive coal deposits and timber stands. At one time Newcastle was the busiest port in Australia. After the California gold rush Newcastle coal was in demand throughout the Pacific. In 1850, 31 000 tons of coal were shipped from Newcastle to the west coast of America.

Lenna, the impressive freestone mansion of Scottish-born shipowner, Alexander McGregor, can be seen through the rigging of the 230-ton intercolonial trader *Natal Queen*. Battery Point, the hilly area behind the wharf, has retained much of its early maritime character to this day. Lenna still stands, having been converted to a restaurant-hotel.

Although Brisbane was declared a port in 1826, the bar at the entrance to the Brisbane River restricted access to ships drawing less than nine feet. Cargo had to be lightered from Moreton Bay anchorage. Approach to the anchorage was then by way of Amity Passage, between Moreton and Stradbroke islands, until the lighthouse was established on Cape Moreton in 1857, and the approach from the north was deepened and buoyed. After Brisbane's separation from the Colony of New South Wales in 1859, the river was progressively deepened until, by 1914, it was deep enough to accommodate any of the ships trading to Australia. This photograph, taken from Bowen Terrace in 1898, shows Howard Smith's Wharf and, beyond the domed Customs House, Australian United Steam Navigation Company's wharf.

By 1850 Brisbane had become a port of entry, with its own Customs House. The imposing 'new' Customs House pictured here demonstrates Brisbane's importance as a port by 1889, the year it was completed.

The first steam train in Australia puffed its way from Melbourne's Flinders Street Station to Hobson's Bay Railway Pier at Sandridge (now Port Melbourne) on 12 September 1854. In this busy scene at Railway Pier in the 1870s, the station train is packed with cargo to be transported to the city centre. Railway Pier, which handled the largest ships in the port, proved too narrow to handle increasing freight, railway and passenger activity. It was eventually demolished to be replaced by Station Pier, which was completed in 1930. A second pier, New Pier (now Princes Pier) had been built west of Railway Pier in 1914.

Five years after Melbourne's first settlement in 1835, Captain Coles bought land fronting the River Yarra and built a wharf between William Street and Spencer Street. Coles' Wharf, later known as Queen's Wharf, was handy to the city, but vessels drawing more than nine feet or exceeding 200 tons had to anchor in Hobson's Bay to lighter their cargo ashore, until deep-water berths were constructed at Sandridge (Port Melbourne). Eventually, at the recommendation of English port engineer, Sir John Coode, the Yarra was straightened, deepened and widened, and Victoria Dock excavated. Queen's Wharf was extended to the entrance of the new Victoria Dock, and became known as North Wharf. South Wharf was built along the opposite bank. The transition from sail to steam can be seen in this photograph of Queen's Wharf.

By the 1850s, Geelong, the nearest port to the Victorian goldfields, vied with Melbourne for import and export cargoes. Here produce is loaded ready for export at Geelong's Yarra Street Pier. The other passenger and cargo-loading terminals were Steamboat and Railway piers.

Sailing ships are berthed on the southern side of Port Adelaide in this photograph taken in 1866. Port Adelaide had been linked with the residential area of the city since 1856 by the first state-owned railway in the British Empire. An inlet on the Gulf St Vincent had first been suggested as the site for settlement by explorer Charles Sturt when he returned to England in 1834. In 1836 surveyor Colonel William Light made the same suggestion; the first settlers arrived in the same year.

By 1882, when this photograph of the New Dock at Port Adelaide was taken, it had become a thriving centre for wool export. In the foreground is the brigantine *Northern Belle*, with the barque *Myrtle Home* beyond. Built at Sunderland in 1875, *Myrtle Home* was sold to Norway in 1908, and renamed the *Glint*. She became a war casualty when she was torpedoed in the North Sea in 1915. Ahead of the barque is the locally-owned *Kebroyd*.

Flags fly from a steamship and a sailing ship, and a small crowd gathers, to commemorate the opening of Port Augusta's new wharf ir 1884. Situated at the head of the Spencer Gulf, Port Augusta became the focal point for an extensive but sparsely-populated pastoral area from which the first shipment of wool for England was loaded in 1859. Deep-water berths for overseas shipping were provided in 1884 with the reclamation of the foreshore. When, eight years later, nearly 50 000 bales of wool were shipped, Port Augusta was dubbed the 'Liverpool of the South'. However, persistent droughts put an end to this reputation. In 1901 only 12 000 bales of wool were loaded. Reprieve came when work began on the Trans-Australian Railway in 1912.

Port Augusta's wide, sleepy Commercial Road looks like the main street of a typical inland township, but for the masts of a big barque projecting above the Port Augusta Hotel. The wharves can be seen at the end of the street in this photograph of 1897. With the decline of the sailing ship era the port became popular with the barques loading wheat. Six such ships could berth at the town wharf to load bagged wheat from stacks on the reclaimed land, or direct from rail trucks.

SALOON
LEWIS
FRUITERER AND SEEDSMAN
BOOT AND SHOE
SMITH & Co

Situated at the mouth of the Swan River, about 20 kilometres downstream from Perth, Fremantle's exposed anchorage and reef-strewn coastal approach were not attractive to shipping, and at first Albany's safe harbour was preferred. However, by 1875, three unloading jetties had been constructed at Fremantle, one of which had been extended to provide a fine-weather berth for ships drawing up to 20 feet. Discovery of gold at Coolgardie in 1892 led to work being resumed on a port within the river. This was opened five years later. By 1899, when this photograph of Fremantle Harbour Wharf was taken, Fremantle had become a thriving port.

This photograph of unidentified ships at Port Darwin was taken in 1892, just four years after the construction of the Darwin-Pine Creek railway, the first in the Territory. Port Darwin was the only navigable harbour in the Northern Territory until mineral deposits were developed at Groote Eylandt and Gove.

# Whalers

Whale oil became Australia's first export when 750 'tuns' left Port Jackson in five ships in 1804. Nine other whaleships, manned by 270 men, were then operating from Sydney. Two years later bay whaling began in Van Diemen's Land, and by the 1860s Hobart was the most important deep-sea whaling base in the British Empire.

Ships used were three-masted barques with up to six whaleboats. Short spars fitted vertically to their topsides protected the wooden hull when whales were brought alongside. Amidships was a deck-house for the boiling cauldrons and furnaces.

Whaleboats were about thirty feet (ten metres) in length, propelled by oars and steered by a longer oar. Key personnel were the headsman and the harpooner. In the bow was a platform just below gunwhale height, with a thigh-board against which the harpooner leant when standing upright to hurl his weapon: a razor-sharp wrought iron harpoon attached to a long line coiled in tubs between the thwarts. When the harpooned whale took off at speed, trailing the line, the perilous and exciting chase began.

Boats were launched when a whale was sighted, silence and speed being essential to get within harpooning range. After the catch was brought alongside blubber was removed with spades and taken aboard to be boiled down, spermacati and oil being retained and the residue used to fuel the furnaces.

Whaling from Hobart extended as far westward as Kerguelen Island; to Albany, Port Lincoln and Twofold Bay on the mainland; and eastward to Norfolk Island, New Zealand and the Auckland and Campbell islands. Eventually steamships with explosive harpoon guns superseded the barques. Shore-based boiling down stations elsewhere brought an end to the Hobart base towards the end of the century.

The last of the Hobart whaling barques, the *Helen*, on the slip in 1894. Eventually steamships with explosive harpoon guns superseded the barques. Towards the end of the century shore-based boiling down stations scattered round the Australian mainland brought an end to the Hobart base.

During the 1860s Hobart was the most important deep-sea whaling base in the British Empire. The *Helen*, pictured unloading 120 tuns of whale oil at Hobart, was the last whaling barque to operate under sail in Tasmania. (A tun is a large cask containing 210 gallons. Ships were originally measured in terms of how many tuns they could stow below deck, hence the origin of tonnage as ships' measurement.) The 343-ton *Helen*, built in Greenock in 1864, was later bought by Alexander McGregor who ran a thriving shipping business based in Hobart.

The *Helen*, seen here arriving at Hobart with boats swung outboard, was a typical whaleship of the day. Usually three-masted barques with up to six whaleboats, these ships had short spars fitted vertically to their topside to protect the wooden hull when whales were brought alongside.

The outlook for these men appears grim as a harpooned whale surfaces under their boat. Shore-based whaling stations around the Australian and New Zealand coasts used clinker-built whaleboats until steam-propelled chasers with harpoon guns took over. Whale boats were double-ended to facilitate backing away after the harpooning and were fitted with a 'loggerhead' at the stern, around which the harpoon line was controlled while it was running out. From the loggerhead the line was taken to a fairlead at the stem that ensured that the boat would always be pulled forwards. Near the loggerhead was a strong leather strap to hold the long oar by which the boat was steered in position. Traditionally, the 'headsman' wielded the lance for the death-blow, while the 'harpooner' took his place at the helm. When a successful chase was over the dead whale was either towed ashore or anchored and allowed to sink. Gases generated inside the body brought it to the surface in a couple of days.

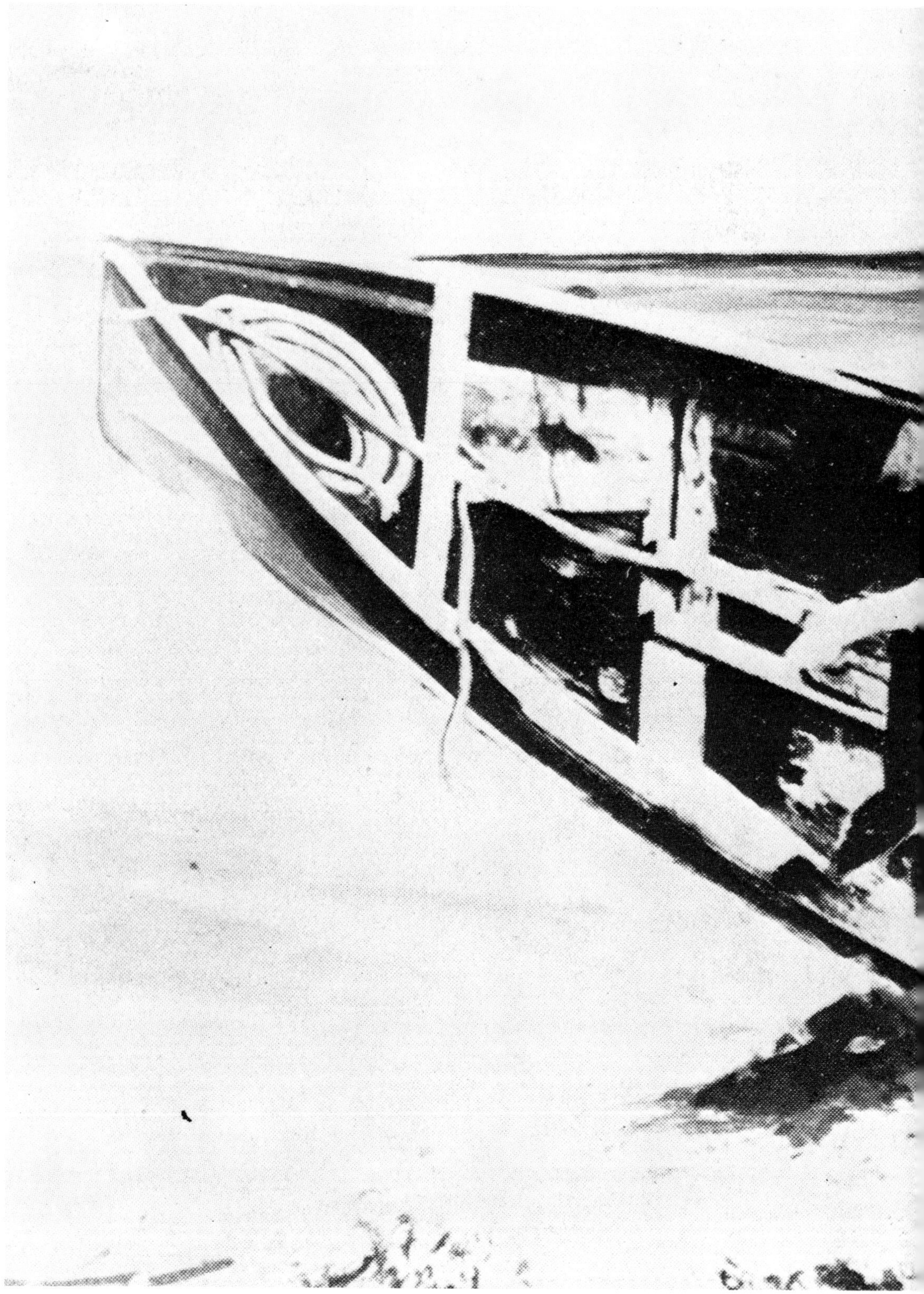

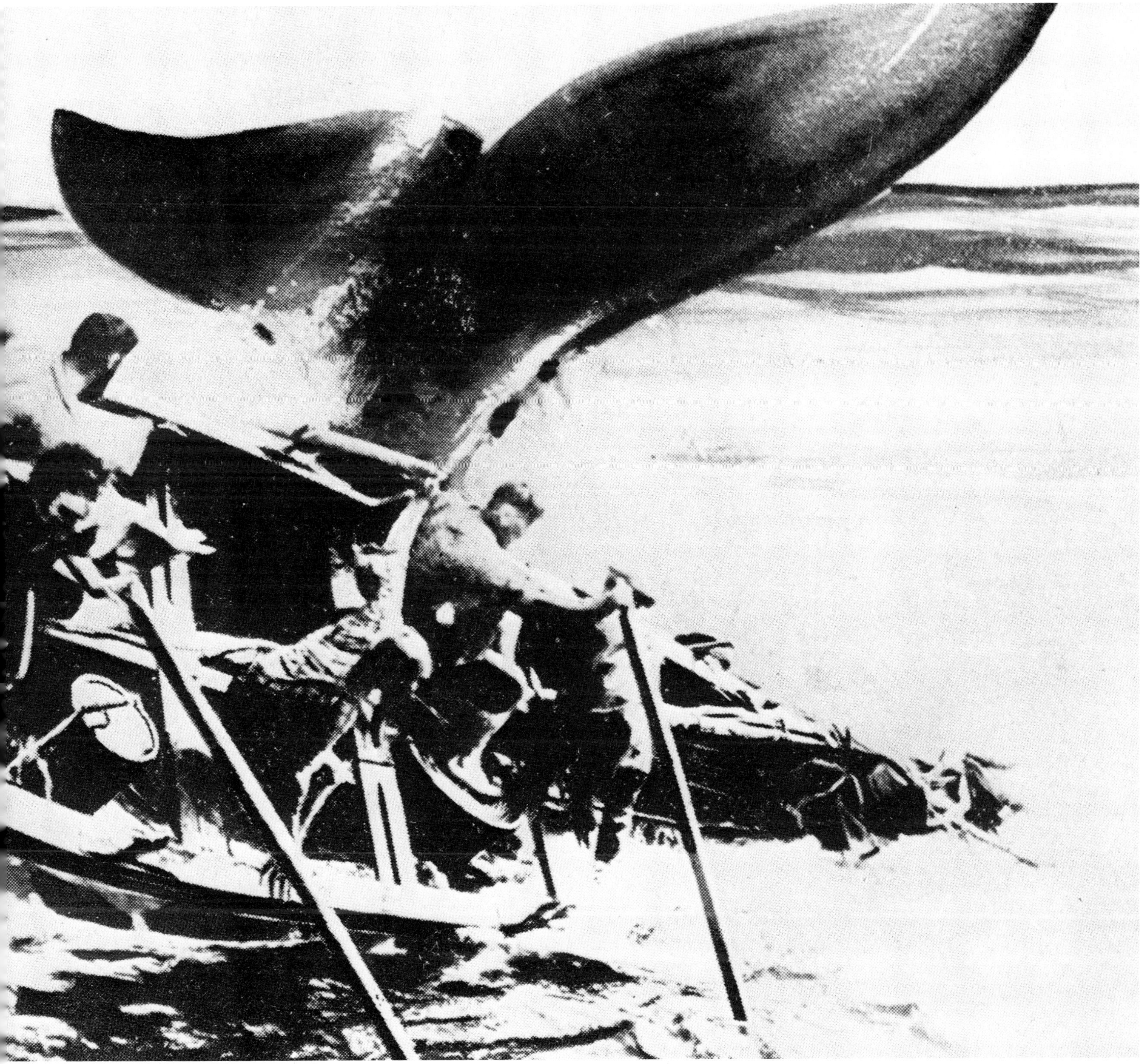

Whales had to be 'cut-in' after being brought alongside the ship. All hands worked with boat spades — sharp blades attached to long handles — used to slice off the blubber in sheets which were taken aboard. When the carcass had been stripped to the waterline it was cut into sections and hauled aboard to complete the de-blubbering. At the trypots the blubber was cut into cubes and boiled, the oil skimmed off into smaller pots to cool before being ladled into casks or tanks. Residue was used as fuel, the whalebone being kept for sale. Here the whaleship *Water Witch* is 'cutting-in' while moored off Hobart Domain in the 1880s. The 236-ton *Water Witch* was acquired by Hobart shipowner Alexander McGregor in 1875 for £1900.

A humpback whale is about to be pulled ashore at Twofold Bay, in southern New South Wales, in this grim photograph. In the 1840s Ben Boyd had established twin townships of East Boyd and Boydtown in Twofold Bay, as a base for his nine whaling ships. One of his employees, Alexander Davidson, established another whaling station at the mouth of the Kiah River, near Boydtown. This remained in operation for 90 years, being run by Davidson's sons and grandsons until 1932, when steam-powered whale-chasers forced them out of business.

The remains of a whale carcass are being stripped of blubber with boat spades in this obviously posed photograph aboard an unknown ship.

The enormous size of trypots, used to boil down whale blubber, is demonstrated by eight children crammed into one, under the watchful eye of the dog. This photograph was taken at a lonely whaling station at Busseltown, Western Australia. Whaling began in that State in 1829.

XIX

# Clippers

Design of sailing ships reached a peak of perfection in clippers. Although developed in response to cut-throat commercial competition, they were extremely beautiful. Their elegance and speed was such that they inspired a mixture of awe and affection in all who saw them.

Seamen vied for positions aboard the most famous clippers, and took great personal pride in keeping them in spanking condition: polishing brasswork, patching sails and touching up paintwork. Even hard-nosed shipowners lavished money on them, ensuring that they would cut a dash whenever they sailed into port. Stories were told about their feats, and wagers laid on the speed of their passages.

Clippers were characterised by slim hulls, graceful bows and lofty masts: all designed for maximum speed. These streamlined square-riggers evolved on both sides of the Atlantic in response to several stimuli: the ending in 1833 of the East India Company's monopoly of trade between England and the Orient; the opening up of the opium and tea trades; the Californian gold rush of 1848 and the Australian gold strikes of the 1850s.

'Clipper' is a somewhat vague term, but it is generally accepted that the first of the American clippers was the 700-ton *Rainbow*, built at New York in 1845. Foremost of the American shipbuilders was Donald McKay of Boston, who built ships for the Californian, China and Australian trades. Several record passages to and from Australia were made by British-owned, American-built ships. 'Composite' clippers with iron frames and wooden planking were a British innovation.

Among the most famous of the clippers to make the 'long haul' to Australia were the *Cutty Sark*, *Thermopylae*, *Sobraon*, *Lightning*, *Torrens* and *Patriach*.

Despite the perfection of clippers they were short-lived as a type, having been constructed over a period of only about thirty years. Steam-propelled ships cut short their glory.

The crew of the *Timaru* proudly pose on the forecastle head of their ship, while berthed at Alfred Graving Dock, Williamstown. Such photographs would be kept as mementoes or sent home to wives and sweethearts. This 1363-ton clipper was built in 1874 for Shaw Savill's Albion Line.

Speed and beauty were the essence of clippers. One of the most famous of them, the *Cutty Sark*, was the fastest wool clipper on the Australian run. Launched in Scotland in 1869 to carry tea from China to London, her career closely paralleled that of rival clipper, the *Thermopylae*. Both ships were of composite iron and wood construction, slightly under 1000 tons, with similar external features. Both began their careers on the China run. Ironically, tea clippers were soon to be ousted by the opening of the Suez Canal, which shortened the journey to the Far East, enabling steamships to compete in the China trade. The *Cutty Sark* and *Thermopylae* were kept on the China run as long as possible. On their earlier voyages, the *Thermopylae* easily outpaced the *Cutty Sark*, but in 1876 the *Cutty Sark's* 64 days to Cape Otway and 72 to Sydney bettered the *Thermopylae's* 74 days to Melbourne. In the subsequent race onwards to Shanghai from Newcastle, the *Cutty Sark* again beat her rival by eight days. Thereafter both ships were exclusively employed in the Australian wool trade. From 1880 to 1885 the *Cutty Sark's* sail area was reduced and she was beaten by less notable craft; but after it had been restored her record 67 days from Sydney to Ushant remained unbeaten, and was again eight days better than the *Thermopylae's*.

The exaggerated, thrusting bow, characteristic of clippers, can clearly be seen in both these photographs of the *Cutty Sark,* now in permanent drydock at Greenwich on the Thames, London. The *Cutty Sark* ended her sailing days under the Portuguese flag. Renamed the *Ferriera*, she was driven ashore in a hurricane off the Florida coast in 1906. After being dismasted in the South Atlantic during World War 1, she was towed to Cape Town. In 1922 she was bought by British sailing ship enthusiast Captain Dowman to be restored to her original rig as a training ship at Falmouth Harbour. After the captain's death his widow donated the clipper to the Thames Nautical Training College. In 1949 the College offered the *Cutty Sark* to the National Maritime Museum. An appeal for funds for restoration brought a world-wide response and, in 1955, the fully restored clipper was opened to the public.

The *Sobraon*, pictured at Sydney's Circular Quay in 1871, was Britain's biggest composite clipper. Teak-planked, with copper fastened to an iron frame, the 2130-ton ship was launched in Glasgow in 1866. She ranked with the *Cutty Sark* and *Thermopylae* for beauty, speed and reliability. Originally intended for the passenger run to China, she was the equivalent of a modern luxury liner. Concerts, deck sports and a ship's newspaper were provided for the amusement of passengers. After the opening of the Suez Canal she joined the England to Australia passenger run under Devitt & Moore's house flag. The *Sobraon's* first voyage to Sydney under Captain Kyle was completed in 75 days, with 78 days homewards. Then, under Captain Elmslie, she made four more voyages to Sydney and between 1871 and 1891, under the same captain, traded only to Melbourne, outwards and homewards via the Cape of Good Hope to avoid the rigours of Cape Horn. She was never hard driven, and broke no records, but earned an excellent reputation with passengers. After discharging at Melbourne on her last outward voyage in December in 1891 the *Sobraon* went on to Sydney where she was permanently moored as a government reformatory ship for boys. (See Chapter 5.)

The last hours of the first and most famous of the American-built clippers for the Australian run, the *Lightning*. This former record-breaking clipper caught fire, loaded with wool and ready to sail from Geelong, on 31 October 1869. After attempts to douse the fire had failed, the ship was moved to an anchorage to protect the pier and other shipping. This photograph was taken after the foremast was destroyed. She later sank about 100 metres offshore. The *Lightning* was built in 1854 by Donald MacKay of Boston for the Liverpool-based Black Ball Line. Under the command of the notorious Captain 'Bully' Forbes, who was reputed to have padlocked the halyards to prevent faint-hearted mates from reducing sail, she made her first round trip from Liverpool to Melbourne in the remarkable time of 160 days, including three weeks in port. She is believed to have made the record day's run for a sailing ship, 436 miles, on her delivery voyage to Liverpool.

The last and one of the most famous of the composite clippers, the *Torrens*, is pictured after colliding with an iceberg. Built at Sunderland in 1875, the *Torrens* was commanded by Captain Angel for fifteen voyages. Fine lines, skysails and fore-topsail studding sails, enabled her to ghost along in the lightest of airs, and she handled the big following seas of the Roaring Forties with ease. Passengers' comfort was always the captain's first consideration, and the *Torrens*, never hard driven, sailed from London every October, calling at Plymouth, and arriving at Adelaide during January, ensuring the best possible weather both ways. Leisurely homeward voyages via the Cape of Good Hope included calls at Cape Town, St Helena and Ascension. Captain Angel's fastest passage was 65 days in 1885, the best day's run 336 miles, and the best recorded speed, fourteen knots. In 1896, Captain Angel's son took command, and on his third voyage the *Torrens* hit an iceberg in the Southern Ocean, limping into Port Adelaide with the bows badly stove in on 5 February 1899. The *Torrens* made her last voyage under the Red Ensign in 1902. She was then sold to Italian owners, and was broken up in Genoa in 1910. The last colonial clipper to carry passengers, the *Torrens* was comparable only with Devitt & Moore's famous *Sobraon*.

The famous *Patriarch* was a familiar sight in Australian ports in the 1870s and 1880s. The first iron ship ordered for the Aberdeen White Star Line, the *Patriarch* was in the Australian wool trade for 24 years, averaging 80 days on outwards passages. Her best homewards passage was 92 days in 1880. Built in 1869, this 1339-ton ship was sold to Norway in 1898, and wrecked on the Argentine coast in 1912.

The mate and stevedore supervisor watch closely as waterside workers finish loading bales of wool into the *Patriarch.* Ballast or deadweight cargo was stowed in the bottom of the hold to ensure stability, and as many bales of wool as possible were then squeezed into the remaining space. To ensure maximum use of the hold, screws were used to compress the bales. If loaded in a wet condition wool cargoes were liable to catch fire through spontaneous combustion.

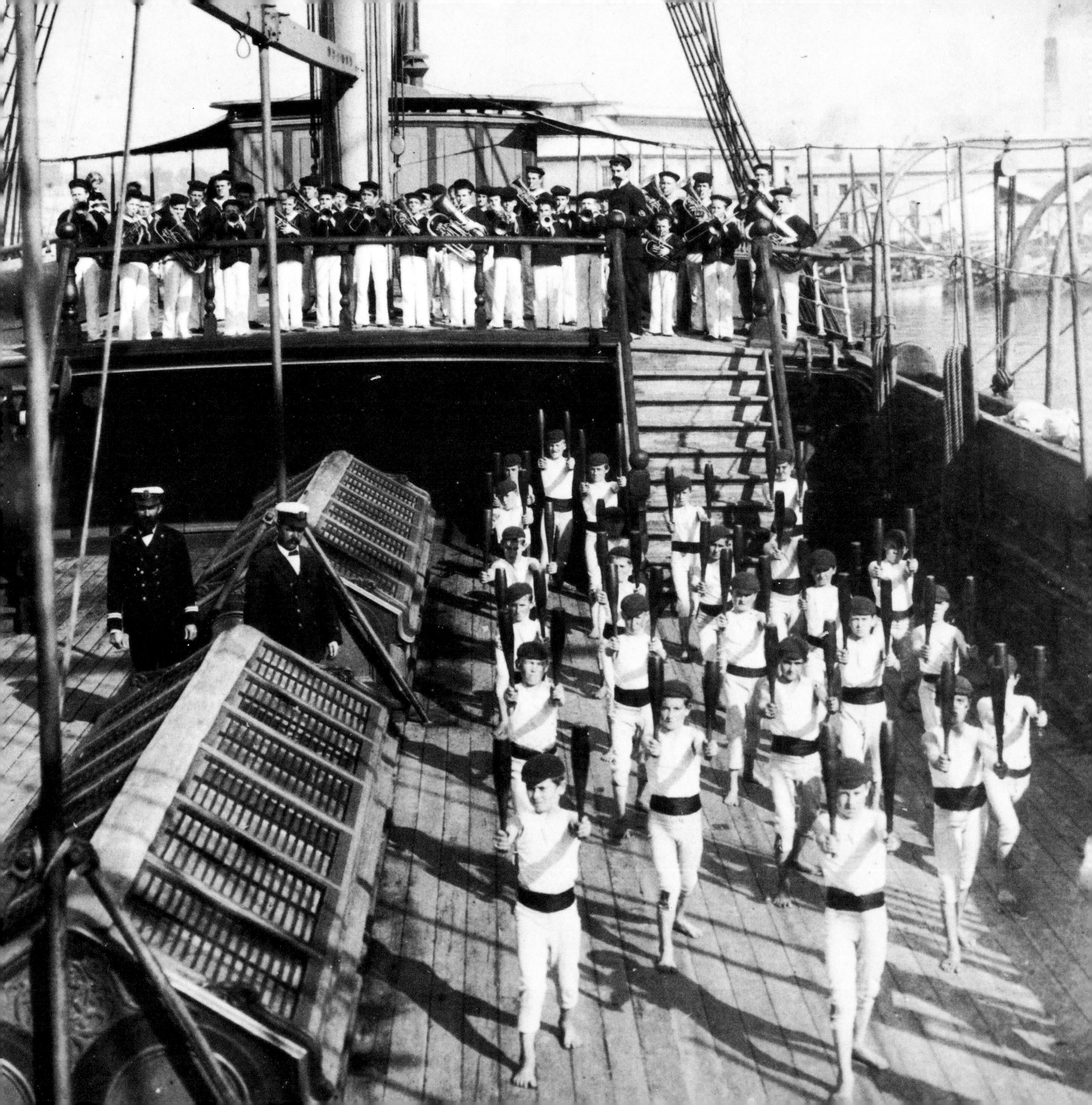

# A Clipper at Rest

The *Sobraon,* one of the most famous ships of her day, ended her life permanently moored in Sydney Harbour. The largest British composite ship ever built, the 2130-ton *Sobraon* was famed for speed and beauty as well as for the luxury of her passenger accommodation. However, with the advent of the steamship her demise as a first-class passenger vessel was inevitable.

In 1890 this graceful clipper made her last voyage to Melbourne where she was ballasted and towed to Sydney. There she was anchored off Cockatoo Island, and fitted out for her new life: that of a reform school ship. (The old sailing ship HMS *Vernon,* previously used to house and train the many homeless boys wandering the streets of Sydney, under a similar scheme, had been destroyed by fire.)

The *Sobraon* was extensively modified for her new task, with school rooms, offices and cabins at either end of the ship. By the time the scheme came to an end, 4000 waifs had passed through the school.

In 1911 the *Sobraon* entered a new phase of her life when the federal government bought her for the sum of $15 000 to be used as a training ship for the newly formed Royal Australian Navy. Refitted once again, she was renamed HMAS *Tingira* and re-anchored at Rose Bay. Boys were trained in signalling and mechanics as well as the art of seamanship. The *Tingira* continued as the Navy's training ship until 30 June 1927 when she was decommissioned. She was later used as a hostel for the unemployed during the Great Depression. When the old ship was finally broken up in 1940 her compositely-constructed hull was still in sound condition.

Boys exercise to the tune of their own brass band on the deck of the *Sobraon*, under the ever-watchful eyes of their instructors.

The staff and nine pupils, with pets, pose aboard the *Sobraon* after it had been converted to a floating reform school for Sydney urchins. The faces of the boys reflect the harshness of their lives before being 'recruited' to the *Sobraon*. Some may have infringed the law, while others were merely homeless. On arrival boys were given a good scrub, a regulation haircut, and issued with a neat sailor's suit. Then, as a symbol of starting a new life, they were asked to throw their old clothes overboard.

Rows of well-scrubbed youngsters are surveyed by the eagle eyes of their instructors in the *Sobraon's* schoolroom. Three teachers from the Department of Public Instruction tutored the boys in the basics of reading, writing and arithmetic, and each boy was taught a trade to fit him for his new life. At the end of their stint aboard the ship boys were placed in a job or the land or in a trade.

Older boys take part in bayonet drill aboard the *Sobraon*. Discipline was strict, with canings and solitary confinement for serious misdemeanors, balanced by a reward system for good behaviour. Skylights to the tween decks are a reminder of the ship's earlier life as a first-class passenger clipper. These skylights once provided light for the luxurious tween deck passenger accommodation.

The entire school seems to be assembled in this deck scene. Playing a musical instrument was one of the many skills that boys had the opportunity to acquire. One of the most famous pupils to emerge from the school was Barney Kieran who, before his 19th birthday, became the top swimmer in the British Empire. Popularly known as the '*Sobraon* wonder boy', he held Australian and world swimming records.

As well as being tutored in academic skills, boys received some training in seamanship while aboard the *Sobraon.* Here they man the yards in a spectacular exercise.

Boys slept sailor-fashion in hammocks slung in a great sweep down the length of the tween deck dormitory. The bell, no doubt used to rouse them at an early hour, was one of several fittings transferred from HMS *Vernon*, an earlier reform ship moored in Sydney Harbour. The composite construction of the ship — wooden decks bolted to iron beams and stringer plates — is clearly visible.

# Coastal and Colonial Traders

The *Alexa*, a graceful little three-masted barquentine, was a familiar sight in New Zealand waters from 1905 to 1912. She was bought by a Wanganui merchant in 1905, traded round the New Zealand coast until 1912, and was then sold to a Chinese merchant employed in Pacific Island trading. From then on the *Alexa* ran between Sydney and the islands until 1929 when she was destroyed by fire in the Gilbert Islands.

From the earliest days of European settlement until the advent of container ships, small sailing vessels traded around Australia, to New Zealand and the Pacific Islands.

Before rail and road transport took over, some carried mail and provisions to far-flung settlements, otherwise cut off from the rest of the world, and transported timber — an invaluable commodity, scarce in the rapidly-expanding colonies — from Tasmania, the northern coast of New South Wales, Maryborough in Queensland, and from remote Western Australian seaports such as Busselton, to Sydney, Melbourne and Adelaide. Others carried timber across the Tasman, often returning to New Zealand with coal from Newcastle.

Exploits of the small island traders between the South Pacific Islands inspired many writers, becoming the subject of a spate of colourful short stories and novels. These traders were involved in a variety of activities, including the guano trade, pearling and the infamous 'labour' trade: the forcible importing of Pacific Islanders to work in Queensland's sugar plantations.

By the first decades of the 20th century, most of Australia's coastal sailing vessels had given way to steamers. Schooners in the Bass Strait timber trade and the ketches of South Australia were the last survivors of the Australian coastal sail traders. The South Australian ketches carried stores to less accessible seaports, returning with wheat and wool to be shipped from larger ports such as Port Lincoln and Port Adelaide.

Sailing vessels remained in the intercolonial trades a little longer, but by the 1920s most of the survivors were operating with auxiliary power.

Blackbirding — the enforced recruitment of natives from the Pacific Islands to work on Queensland sugar plantations — was on the wane when this photograph was taken of the 247-ton barquentine *May* in 1892. She is ready to sail from Bundaberg, Queensland, to repatriate islanders whose contracts had expired. Commonwealth legislation prohibited the entry of native labour after 1904, and arranged for the repatriation of many Kanaks. The *May* was sold to New Zealand owners in 1898. Thereafter she was used in the timber trade until wrecked on the Kaipara bar in 1902.

The *Ilma*, a 345-ton barquentine, was one of the smaller ships involved in the intercolonial trade. She was built at Greenock for Norwegian owners, but was registered at Liverpool under the ownership of the British and Mexican Shipping Company from 1892 until 1903, when she was acquired by Auckland owners for the intercolonial trade. From 1911 until 1917 she was a coal hulk at Hobart; but was recommissioned as a barque for two years during the wartime shipping shortage. She was again hulked at Auckland in 1919, towed to Wellington in 1922, and eventually scuttled in Cook Strait in 1937.

The *Huia* was the last sailing ship to be used in the trans-Tasman trade. A wooden topsail schooner built on Kaipara Harbour in 1894, she was later fitted with an auxiliary engine. The *Huia* is credited with some of the fastest sailing ship passages between Australia and New Zealand, and remained in the trade until 1950 when she was transferred to Fijian registry. Soon after leaving Noumea in January 1952 she ran aground on Komekame Reef. Fire broke out after the cargo had been salvaged, and the wreck was eventually destroyed in a cyclone.

The *Helen Denny*, a 727-ton iron ship built by Duncans of Port Glasgow in 1866, was noted for speed. When sold to Shaw Savill & Co. for the New Zealand emigrant trade in 1875 her fastest outward passage was 82 days to Lyttelton. In 1896 the *Helen Denny* was sold to Turnbull & Co. of Christchurch for the intercolonial trade, and in 1901 was cut down to a barque after being resold to Captain F. Holm. In 1913 she was hulked at Wellington, and later saw similar service at Lyttelton and Auckland before eventually being scuttled off Cuvier Island, near Auckland, in 1948. She is pictured at Port Chalmers, Otago Harbour.

The elegant, three-masted iron barque *Laira*, photographed during a low-spot in her long career. On 2 April 1898 she was loading wool at Dunedin when the Union Steamship Company's *Wakatipu* ran into her. She sunk before helpless onlookers in ten minutes. Refloated three weeks later, the wool was unloaded and she resumed her career around Australasian waters. Built in Sunderland in 1870, and registered at Plymouth, her registration had been transferred to Auckland in 1882. In 1909 she was bought by Huddart Parker & Co. for use as a coal hulk in the River Yarra, Melbourne. She was broken up in the 1950s.

Described as 'the prettiest vessel ever launched in Belfast', the *Polly Woodside* (top) was a typical small merchant sailing ship of her era. Christened by her namesake Mrs Polly Woodside on 7 November 1885, she was launched from the slipway of Workman Clark & Co. Although this small deep-water, square-rigged sailing ship was designed for maximum cargo capacity, she had the fine lines of a clipper. After being engaged in the South American trade for many years — outward with coal and returning with nitrates — she was sold to New Zealand owners in 1903. Renamed the *Rona*, she traded first across the Tasman to Australia, and later to the United States. In the bottom photograph she is pictured during her long career as an intercolonial trader.

By 1930 the *Rona* had suffered the ignoble fate of many old sailing vessels: conversion into a coal hulk. By 1962, she was one of the last former sailing ships still afloat in Australia, albeit in the truncated, rusty and filthy state shown here. She has since been restored to her original splendour.

The restoration of the *Polly Woodside*, pictured on the Yarra River, Melbourne, where she is now the centrepiece of a maritime museum, was the result of more than sixteen years of voluntary labour led by Captain Gerry Heyen and supported by the State Government, the National Trust of Australia (Victoria), commercial enterprises and a dedicated and hard-working band of devotees. Captain Heyen's lifelong experience at sea had included a stint aboard *Rothesay Bay*, a near sister-ship to the *Polly Woodside*. He later served as mate and master of the 334-ton steel barquentine *Alexa*. Shortly before Captain Heyen died at the age of 80 he saw the result of his efforts: the rusty wreck of the *Rona* restored as the beautiful barque *Polly Woodside*.

The *James Craig*, pictured during her days as an intercolonial trader, is another small iron barque to be resurrected after the degradation of becoming a rusty coal hulk. Originally named *Clan Macleod*, the 671-ton barque was built at Sunderland in 1874. At about the turn of the century she was renamed when she was acquired by J.J. Craig of Auckland for the intercolonial trade. The *James Craig* was eventually abandoned at Recherche Bay, southern Tasmania, after service as a coal hulk. Subsequent restoration was the work of a group of enthusiasts who founded the Sydney Cove Maritime Museum in 1965. In 1973 the *James Craig* was towed to Hobart where her hull was made sufficiently seaworthy for the longer tow to Sydney. In 1981 her restoration was completed at Birkenhead Point, Sydney, with the help of a federal government grant of $10 000.

The *Alma Doepel*, pictured in her heyday, is the sole survivor of the sailing ships built on the banks of the Bellinger River in northern New South Wales to transport timber from the area. This 118-foot long, three-masted topsail schooner with a sliding keel was launched at Bellingen on 10 October 1903. She was used in the timber trade until 1917 when she was bought by Henry Jones of Hobart for the Bass Strait run. Her record sailing time was 58½ hours from Hobart to Port Phillip in 1937. During World War 2 she was the last surviving Australian-built topsail schooner to carry square-sails when the yards were removed and, with diesel auxiliaries, she became AK 82, an army supply ship in New Guinea waters. After the war the *Alma Doepel* resumed trading across Bass Strait, without square-sails, but during the 1960s was relegated to a limestone carrier on the Derwent River.

The *Alma Doepel* as she is today, photographed at Melbourne's Victoria Dock. Her transformation from a single-masted hulk began when Melbourne yachtsman Michael Wood realised her potential for restoration. A non-profit-making organisation, Sail and Adventure Ltd, acquired the hulk for the scrap value of her diesel engines which were serviceable enough to get her to Melbourne. Melbourne Harbour Trust Commissioners, now the Port of Melbourne Authority, allotted one of their little-used berths and adjacent wharf sheds for workshops and storage. The Alma Doepel Supporters Club was formed and attracted willing helpers, including experienced shipwrights, riggers, sailmakers, engineers and young but enthusiastic novices. Sponsorship was forthcoming from several business houses. By 1981 the masts and rigging had been restored and during the next year the hull and sliding keel housing were made as good as new. Square-sail yards were in position by 1983, and for her 80th birthday the *Alma* received a new suit of sails. With a regular crew of nine, and Supporters Club trainees, accommodation is being installed that will enable the *Alma Doepel* to make regular ten-day youth voyages in and from Port Phillip, and occasional voyages interstate with Captain Wood at the helm.

# The Last of the Cape Horners

The 19th century cast long shadows into the 20th century, and a few big European-owned windjammers survived until the 1930s. Amazingly, two, the *Pamir* and *Passat,* made their last race round Cape Horn in 1949.

The last of the Cape Horners carried homeward cargoes of wool and wheat, for which fast passages were less important than operating costs. These were kept in check by cutting full-rigged ships back to barques, thus reducing sail-handling. The majority of the more recently-built ships were barque-rigged.

Before the completion of the Panama Canal, sail still had the advantage over steam on the homeward run around Cape Horn, where steamships were hampered by the lack of coaling stations. The opening of the Panama Canal in 1913 disadvantaged the few surviving windjammers, just as half a century earlier the Suez Canal had ousted sailing ships from the Far Eastern routes.

One man dominated the saga of the last days of the Cape Horners: Captain Gustaf Erikson. Erikson was a native of the Aland Islands which lie between Finland and Sweden on the Gulf of Bothnia. At the time of his birth in 1872, sailing ships were at the peak of perfection. At the age of ten Gustaf went to sea as a cabin boy in ships owned and commanded by his relations and, ten years later, was in command of *Adele* in the Baltic timber trade. Because he was not qualified, he was accompanied by a sailing master. When he obtained his master's certificate in 1900, and took command of the *Southern Belle* in the same trade, he received a meagre salary plus 5 per cent commission on the freight and charter parties he negotiated with brokers, experience that was to prove invaluable when he became a shipowner.

Captain Erikson gained foreign-going expertise in command of the ship *Albania* in 1905, taking coal from South Wales to South America and bringing back timber from the Gulf of Mexico. He later went into partnership with his relatives to buy the Dutch-built composite barque *Tjerimai,* and by 1917 the partners owned seven big ships including the 2816-ton *Lawhill.*

After World War 1, Captain Erikson bought up several large sailing ships at scrap-metal prices, which he used to carry grain from Australia to Europe. Several of his ships, beautiful but anachronistic survivors of a now vanished tradition, can be seen on the following pages.

The four-masted barque *Pamir* was the best known of the last big sailing ships in Australian waters. She had a long and colourful history which ended on 21 September 1957 when she capsized in a storm in the North Atlantic, with a loss of 80 lives. Six survivors were picked up from lifeboats the next day. The *Pamir* was built by Blohm and Voss for the Chilean nitrate trade in 1905. Soon after the outbreak of World War 1 she was interned in the Canary Islands, and eventually allocated to Italy under reparations. In 1931 she was bought by Captain Erikson, and traded to Australia and New Zealand until 1941 when she was seized at Wellington as a war prize. She later traded between New Zealand and America and Canada under New Zealand registration. In March 1948, she made an historic voyage to London under an all-New Zealand crew. After her return to Wellington the British Government decided that all seized ships should be given back to Finland, and the *Pamir* was restored to the Erikson fleet.

The 1903-ton *Mount Stewart* and her identical sister-ship *Cromdale* were built at Glasgow in 1891, the last British full-rigged ships built for the Australian run. In 1913, returning from South America with nitrate, the *Cromdale* was wrecked in fog while making a landfall near the Lizard Light on the Cornish coast. The *Mount Stewart* survived till the late 1920s to become the last big British sailing ship to fly the Red Ensign.

The *Olivebank*, 2818 tons, was built in Scotland in 1892. In 1915 she was sold to Norwegian owners, changing hands several times before becoming one of Gustaf Erikson's fleet of grain carriers in 1924. She took part in most of the subsequent wheat races, but was not particularly notable for speed. In 1939, bound for her home port of Mariehamn, Finland, she became one of the first casualties of World War 2. She sank in the North Sea after striking a mine, only seven of her crew surving.

Originally built for the Belgian government as a training ship, *L'Avenir* was bought by Gustaf Erikson in 1932, and took part in the grain races from South Australia to Europe for the next five years. In 1937 Erikson sold her to the German Hamburg-Amerika Line. As the *Admiral Karpfanger* she was used both as a cadet ship and grain carrier until 1938, when she disappeared, apparently foundering off Cape Horn. Her last shortwave radio communication with Germany was on 1 March when she reported her position to be 200 nautical miles south of New Zealand and all well. Eventually, wreckage found on Wollaston Island, near Cape Horn, was identified.

L'Avenir

The *Hougomont*, eventually to become another of Erikson's grain ships, was built for Hardie's of Glasgow in 1897. Captain Erikson bought the *Hougomont* for £3500 in 1925. In October 1927, loaded with timber for Melbourne, all the sails were blown out in an Atlantic gale and the ship had to be towed into Lisbon for repairs. Final disaster came in 1932, in the Great Australian Bight, when the *Hougomont* was bound for the Spencer Gulf in ballast. Caught in a sudden Southern Ocean storm, all four masts went overboard. Captain Lindholm ordered jury sails to be rigged on the four stumps and sailed on to Adelaide, refusing assistance from passing steamships, thereby avoiding salvage costs for Captain Erikson. The *Hougomont* was not insured, and re-rigging would have cost more than the ship was worth. There were no offers for the hull which was eventually used as a breakwater at Stenhouse Bay, at the southern tip of Yorke Peninsula where she still lies.

The *Lord Shaftesbury*, a four-masted barque of 2341 tons, was built for British owners in 1888, flying the Red Ensign until 1915. When rounding Cape Horn in 1912 a huge wave swept away her boats and deckhouse, drowning a seaman. Days after this she seemed doomed when she became trapped in ice but her master managed to free her. In 1915 the *Lord Shaftesbury* was renamed the *Golden Gate* after being sold to San Fransisco owners. She was broken up in 1934.

The *Lawhill*, the last of the big sailing ships to call at Melbourne, first arrived there in 1919 as part of Captain Erikson's fleet, making the outward voyage in 99 days, and returning homeward, with wheat loaded at Geelong, in 96 days. She then traded world-wide for Erikson until 13 April 1941 when she was seized as a war prize by the British, Norway having been invaded by the Germans through Finland. Thereafter, she was operated by the South African government between Australia and South Africa, retaining her Finnish crew. She was in the Port of Melbourne for the last time on 31 May 1943. After the war she was left derelict at Lourenco Marques, East Africa.

These deck scenes aboard the *Pamir* are among the last photographs of the ship in Australian waters. On 1 February 1949 the *Pamir* left Wellington for the Spencer Gulf, South Australia, where she was loaded with wheat for her last race home against her sister-ship, the *Passat*. By losing this historic race the *Pamir* became the last commercial sailing ship to round Cape Horn. After unloading, both ships went to their home port of Mariehamn, Finland, to lay up. In 1951 they were sold for breaking up but were reprieved when they were bought by a West German company for conversion into cadet training ships. Auxiliary engines were added. By the 1950s the *Pamir* and *Passat* were the world's last deep-sea sailing ships still in operation. Soon after the *Pamir* had capsized and sunk in a storm west of the Azores in 1957, the *Passat* ran into difficulties, and had to put into Lisbon. She is now permanently moored at Travenmunde, Germany, where she has been preserved as a training ship and youth hostel.

Among the last in a brave tradition, topmen secure sails aboard the *Pamir* in both these photographs. This job was particularly precarious in stormy conditions. One slip meant almost certain death.

This aerial view of the *Pamir*, the last of the Cape Horners, was taken off Sydney Heads *en route* to Wellington in about 1947.

*They mark our passage as a race of men*
*Earth will not see such ships as those again.*
John Mansfield

# Acknowledgements

Compiling the text for this book involved the study of previously published accounts, and invaluable assistance in this respect was rendered by Ned Stonehouse, the Point Lonsdale lighthouse-keeper, who consulted his extensive library of sailing ship volumes; and by the unnamed typist who copied his notes. Ned's library includes Basil Lubbock's *Colonial Clippers* and *Last of the Windjammers*, from which he extracted details about *Torrens*, *Helen Denny*, *Mount Stewart*, *Sobraon* and other ships. Harry O'May's *Wooden Hookers of Hobart* and Will Lawson's *Bluegum Clippers and Whaleships of Tasmania* were also consulted, and *Era of the Clipper Ships* revealed the *Golden Gate* story.

Ship and port histories were taken from my books — *Hazards of the Sea*, *Port Phillip Pilots and Defences* and *Port Phillip Panorama* — and from John Bach's *Maritime History of Australia*. Tom Mead's *Killers of Eden* provided some of the stories on whaling.

Ingram and Wheatley's *Shipwrecks — New Zealand Disasters* is the source of earlier New Zealand incidents, and Jack Churchouse's *The Pamir* gives more recent stories from across the Tasman Sea. Finally, *Shipping Wonders of the World* and *The Oxford Companion to Ships and the Sea* constantly supplemented my seafaring knowledge and experience.

JOHN NOBLE

# Pictorial Acknowledgements

The Publishers and author would like to thank the following organisations for permission to reproduce photographs from their collections.

Adelaide *Advertiser* pages 53, 104, 106, 112, 113.
Australian Consolidated Press, Tyrell Collection page 66.
Herald and Weekly Times Limited pages 4, 70, 71, 76, 103, 111.
Maritime Museum of Tasmania page 64.
Melbourne Maritime Museum pages 98 (top), 99, 100.
National Library of Australia pages 22, 35, 46, 47, 48-49, 50, 52, 61, 62-63, 65, 77.
National Library of New Zealand, Alexander Turnbull Library, Wellington pages 33, 68, 90, 94, 95, 96, 97, 98 (bottom), 101, 102, 108, 109, 114, 116.
New South Wales Government Printing Office pages 38, 41, 72-73, 78, 80-81, 82-83, 84-85, 86, 87, 88-89.
Royal Historical Society of Queensland pages 92-93.
Royal Western Australian Historical Society pages 56, 67.
State Library of New South Wales, Mitchell Library pages 20, 40.
State Library of South Australia, A. D. Edwardes Collection pages 3, 6, 7, 8-9, 10, 11, 15, 18, 19, 23, 24-25, 27, 28-29, 30, 31, 32, 36, 39, 54, 57, 74, 115; South Australian Archives page 55.
State Library of Tasmania, W. L. Crowther Library pages 45, 58, 66.
State Library of Victoria, La Trobe Library pages x, 5, 12, 13, 14, 16-17, 26, 51, 75.
West Australian Newspapers Ltd page 2.